MW00895842

Key to
Wren's
New Shorter
English Grammar

6

S. CHAND & COMPANY

(An ISO 9001 : 2000 Company)
RAM NAGAR, NEW DELHI - 110 055

Sole Distributors :

S. CHAND & COMPANY LTD.

(An ISO 9001 : 2000 Company)

Head Office: 7361, RAM NAGAR, NEW DELHI - 110 055
Phone: 23672080-81-82, 9899107446, 9911310888
Fax: 91-11-23677446
Shop at: schandgroup.com; e-mail: info@schandgroup.com

Branches :

AHMEDABAD : 1st Floor, Heritage, Near Gujarat Vidhyapeeth, Ashram Road, **Ahmedabad** - 380 014, Ph: 27541965, 27542369, ahmedabad@schandgroup.com

BANGALORE : No. 6, Ahuja Chambers, 1st Cross, Kumara Krupa Road, **Bangalore** - 560 001, Ph: 22268048, 22354008, bangalore@schandgroup.com

BHOPAL : 238-A, M.P. Nagar, Zone 1, **Bhopal** - 462 011, Ph: 4274723. bhopal@schandgroup.com

CHANDIGARH : S.C.O. 2419-20, First Floor, Sector - 22-C (Near Aroma Hotel), **Chandigarh** -160 022, Ph: 2725443, 2725446, chandigarh@schandgroup.com

CHENNAI : 152, Anna Salai, **Chennai** - 600 002, Ph: 28460026, chennai@schandgroup.com

COIMBATORE : Plot No. 5, Rajalakshmi Nagar, Peelamedu, **Coimbatore** -641 004, (M) 09444228242, coimbatore@schandgroup.com

CUTTACK : 1st Floor, Bhartia Tower, Badambadi, **Cuttack** - 753 009, Ph: 2332580; 2332581, cuttack@schandgroup.com

DEHRADUN : 1st Floor, 20, New Road, Near Dwarka Store, **Dehradun** - 248 001, Ph: 2711101, 2710861, dehradun@schandgroup.com

GUWAHATI : Pan Bazar, **Guwahati** - 781 001, Ph: 2738811, 2735640 guwahati@schandgroup.com

HYDERABAD : Sultan Bazar, **Hyderabad** - 500 195, Ph: 24651135, 24744815, hyderabad@schandgroup.com

JAIPUR : A-14, Janta Store Shopping Complex, University Marg, Bapu Nagar, **Jaipur** - 302 015, Ph: 2719126, jaipur@schandgroup.com

JALANDHAR : Mai Hiran Gate, **Jalandhar** - 144 008, Ph: 2401630, 5000630, jalandhar@schandgroup.com

JAMMU : 67/B, B-Block, Gandhi Nagar, **Jammu** - 180 004, (M) 09878651464

KOCHI : Kachapilly Square, Mullassery Canal Road, Ernakulam, **Kochi** - 682 011, Ph: 2378207, cochin@schandgroup.com

KOLKATA : 285/J, Bipin Bihari Ganguli Street, **Kolkata** - 700 012, Ph: 22367459, 22373914, kolkata@schandgroup.com

LUCKNOW : Mahabeer Market, 25 Gwynne Road, Aminabad, **Lucknow** - 226 018, Ph: 2626801, 2284815, lucknow@schandgroup.com

MUMBAI : Blackie House, 103/5, Walchand Hirachand Marg, Opp. G.P.O., **Mumbai** - 400 001, Ph: 22690881, 22610885, mumbai@schandgroup.com

NAGPUR : Karnal Bag, Model Mill Chowk, Umrer Road, **Nagpur** - 440 032, Ph: 2723901, 2777666 nagpur@schandgroup.com

PATNA : 104, Citicentre Ashok, Govind Mitra Road, **Patna** - 800 004, Ph: 2300489, 2302100, patna@schandgroup.com

PUNE : 291/1, Ganesh Gayatri Complex, 1st Floor, Somwarpeth, Near Jain Mandir, **Pune** - 411 011, Ph: 64017298, pune@schandgroup.com

RAIPUR : Kailash Residency, Plot No. 4B, Bottle House Road, Shankar Nagar, **Raipur** - 492 007, Ph: 09981200834, raipur@schandgroup.com

RANCHI : Flat No. 104, Sri Draupadi Smriti Apartments, East of Jaipal Singh Stadium, Neel Ratan Street, Upper Bazar, **Ranchi** - 834 001, Ph: 2208761, ranchi@schandgroup.com

VISAKHAPATNAM : Plot No. 7, 1st Floor, Allipuram Extension, Opp. Radhakrishna Towers, Seethammadhara North Extn., **Visakhapatnam** - 530 013, (M) 09347580841, visakhapatnam@schandgroup.com

ISBN : 81-219-2705-6   **Code** : 11 983

PRINTED IN INDIA
*By Rajendra Ravindra Printers Pvt. Ltd., 7361, Ram Nagar, New Delhi -110 055
and published by S. Chand & Company, 7361, Ram Nagar, New Delhi -110 055.*

CHAPTER 2 SUBJECT AND PREDICATE

EXERCISE

Subject	Predicate
1. The boy	stood on the burning deck
2. Stone walls	do not a prison make
3. The singing of the birds	delights us
4. Bad habits	grow unconsciously
5. Edison	invented the phonograph
6. We	cannot pump the ocean dry

CHAPTER 3 THE PHRASE AND THE CLAUSE

EXERCISE

1. Open the book at page 24 .
2. How hot it is !
3. Have you ever heard about Kumbhakarna ?
4. Turn the TV down .
5. What channel is the programme on ?
6. The moon goes round the earth .
7. What a lovely garden !
8. Read the instructions carefully .
9. Can you lend me your DVD player ?
10. I got the information from the internet .
11. There is a phone message for you .
12. How useful the computer is !

CHAPTER 4 PARTS OF SPEECH

EXERCISE

Still (1)	Adjective	qualifies	'waters' Noun
Still (2)	Adverb	modifies	'lives' Verb
After (3)	Preposition	governs	'storm' Noun
After (4)	Adjective	qualifies	'effects' Noun

Note : Number in bracket refers to the corresponding sentence number.

up (5)	Adjective	qualifies	'train' Noun
about (6)	Adverb	modifies	'weighs' Verb
about (7)	Preposition	governs	'battle' Noun
off (8)	Preposition	governs	'me' Pronoun
off (9)	Adverb	modifies	'came' Verb
fast (10)	Verb	Predicate	Mohammadans - Subject

CHAPTER 5 THE NOUN : KINDS OF NOUNS

EXERCISE 1

Common	Proper	Collective	Abstract
bank, year (5)	Nile (5)	crowd (1)	truth (2)
ships, harbour(4)	Nelson, (7)	fleet (4)	cleanliness,
five (6)	Trafalgar	committee (6)	godliness (3)
		team (9)	victory (7)
			voice (8)
			lie (10)

EXERCISE 2

1. lazy - laziness
2. cruel - cruelty
3. brave - bravery
4. foolish - foolishness

EXERCISE 3

A.

Adjective	Abstract Noun	Adjective	Abstract Noun
long (1)	length	young (2)	youth
humble (3)	humility	decent (4)	decency
strong (5)	strength	true (6)	truth
short (7)	shortage	prudent (8)	prudence
wide (9)	width	wise (10)	wisdom
good (11)	goodness	vacant (12)	vacancy
broad (13)	breadth	free (14)	freedom
proud (15)	pride	brave (16)	bravery
high (17)	height	poor (18)	poverty
just (19)	justice	vain (20)	vanity

B.

Verb	Abstract Noun	Verb	Abstract Noun
Laugh (1)	Laughter	Obey (2)	Obedience
Live (3)	Livelihood	Expect (4)	Expectation

Note : Number in bracket refers to the corresponding sentence number.

Excel (5)	Excellence	Believe (6)	Belief
Serve (7)	Service	Hate (8)	Hatred
Please (9)	Pleasure	Act (10)	Action
Choose (11)	Choice	Move (12)	Movement
Conceal (13)	Concealment	Seize (14)	Seizure
Flatter (15)	Flattery	Defend (16)	Defence
Think (17)	Thought	Protect (18)	Protection
Advise (19)	Advice	Punish (20)	Punishment
Free (21)	Freedom	See (22)	Sight
Judge (23)	Judgement	Relieve (24)	Relief
Pursue (25)	Pursuit		

C.

Common Noun	Abstract Noun	Common Noun	Abstract Noun
King (1)	Kingdom	Man (2)	Manhood, Mankind
Thief (3)	Theft	Woman (4)	Womanhood
Infant (5)	Infancy	Owner (6)	Ownership
Rogue (7)	Roguery	Regent (8)	Regency
Mother (9)	Motherhood	Agent (10)	Agency
Hero (11)	Heroism	Beggar (12)	Beggary
Priest (13)	Priesthood	Boy (14)	Boyhood
Bond (15)	Bondage	Pirate (16)	Piracy
Friend (18)	Friendship	Captain (18)	Captainship, Captaincy
Rascal (19)	Rascality	Patriot (20)	Patriotism

EXERCISE 4

Countable Nouns	Uncountable Nouns
puri (2)	rice (1)
garden (5)	flour (3)
sweater (8)	water (4)
song (9)	honesty (6)
suitcase (12)	wool (7)
luggage (13)	music (10)
jar (15)	climate (11)
	honey (14)

Note : Number in bracket refers to the corresponding sentence number.

CHAPTER 8 THE NOUN — CASE

EXERCISE

Nominative Case	Accusative Case	Possessive Case
players (3)	the boy (1)	uncle's home (2)
students (5)	kite (4)	Nature's laws (6)
	window (7)	girls' (8)
	me (9)	legs of the table (10)

Note : Number in bracket refers to the corresponding sentence number.

CHAPTER 9 THE ADJECTIVE

EXERCISE

1. heavy - Adj. of quality
2. every - Distributive Adjective
3. live, dead - Adj. of quality
4. neither - Distributive Numeral
5. what - Interrogative Adj.
6. which - Interrogative Adj.
   next - Adj. ordinals or Demonstrative Adj.
7. second - Def. Numeral Adj.
8. my - Possessive Adj.
9. some - Adj. of Number
10. Much, little - Adj. of quantity
11. good - Adj. of quality

CHAPTER 10 COMPARISON OF ADJECTIVES

EXERCISE 1

Positive	Comparative	Superlative
Black	Blacker	Blackest
Excellent	More excellent	most excellent
Ill	worse	worst
Gloomy	Gloomier	Gloomiest
Mad	madder	Maddest
Safe	safer	safest
Bad	worse	worst
Unjust	more unjust	most unjust
Gay	gayer	gayest
Able	abler	ablest

Dry	drier	driest
Timid	more timid	most timid
Ugly	uglier	ugliest
True	truer	truest
Severe	more severe	most severe
Exact	more exact	most exact
Agreeable	more agreeable	most agreeable
Difficult	more difficult	most difficult
Little	less, lesser	least
Few	fewer	fewest
Numerous	more numerous	most numerous
Merry	merrier	merriest

EXERCISE 2

(a) 1. latter   2. later   3. later
(b) 1. elder   2. older   3. elder
(c) 1. oldest   2. oldest   3. eldest
(d) 1. latest   2. last   3. last
(e) 1. nearest   2. next   3. nearest

EXERCISE 3

Comparative	Superlative	Positive
1. happier	5. wisest	1. poor
2. less	6. best	3. slight
4. stronger		7. good
8. sharper		

EXERCISE 4

Positive	Comparative	Superlative
shameful	more shameful	most shameful
clever	cleverer	cleverest
pretty	prettier	prettiest
interesting	more interesting	most interesting
hopeful	more hopeful	most hopeful
honest	more honest	most honest

EXERCISE 5

A. 1. better   **2.** idlest   **3.** sharper
    4. older   **5.** best   **6.** worse, worst

EXERCISE 6

B. 1. better   **2.** mightier   **3.** better   **4.** whiter
5. fastest   **6.** highest   **7.** better   **8.** highest
9. costier   **10.** tallest

EXERCISE 7

1. The pine apple is less sweeter than mango.
2. Gold is less plentiful than silver.
3. Copper is less useful than iron.

EXERCISE 8

1. No other democracy in the world is as *large* as India.   **Positive**
   India is *larger* democracy than any other in the world. **Comparative**
2. Meat is not *more nutritious* than some beans. **Comparative**
3. Latiff is *more industrious* than most other boys. **Comparative**
   Latiff is one of the *most Industrious* boys. **Superlative**
4. He would die soon than tell a lie. **Positive**
5. Very few Indian kings were as *great* as Samudra Gupta. **Positive**
   Samudra Gupta was *greater* than most other Indian kings. **Comparative**
6. The tiger is *more ferocious* than any other animal. **Comparative**
   No other animal is so *ferocious* as the Tiger. **Positive**
7. Lead is the *heaviest* metal. **Superlative**
   No other metal is as *heavy* as lead. **Comparative**

CHAPTER 11 MORE ABOUT ADJECTIVES

EXERCISE 1

1. A strange young girl   2. funny old buildings
3. A nice, new, blue sari   4. A tall young American tourist
5. old brown leather shoes   6. black nylon swimming trunks

EXERCISE 2

1. the little   2. a little   3. a little

EXERCISE 3

1. a few 　　　　**2.** the few 　　　　**3.** a few
4. a few 　　　　**5.** the few 　　　　**6.** a few

CHAPTER 12 ADJECTIVE PHRASES

EXERCISE 1

1. The rise is a flower of beauty.

2. A man of courage does not fear danger.

3. Deeds of heroism deserve our admiration.

4. Much has been said about the scenery of Switzerland.

EXERCISE 2

1. Some of the buildings in New York are very high.

2. Nelson was a fearless boy.

3. It was a very beautiful sunset.

4. Nobody likes a temperamental person.

CHAPTER 13 ARTICLES

EXERCISE 1

1. a 　　**2.** an 　　**3.** the 　　**4.** the 　　**5.** a
6. an 　　**7.** the 　　**8.** a 　　**9.** the 　　**10.** an

EXERCISE 2

A.

1. While there is a life, there is hope.

2. The Sun rises in the east.

3. The brave soldier lost an arm in the battle.

4. The doctor says it is a hopeless case.

5. I like to live in the open air.

6. Get a pound of sugar from the nearest grocer.

7. Set back the clock; it is an hour too fast.

8. You must take a care.

CHAPTER **14** PERSONAL PRONOUNS

EXERCISE 1

1. she (Alice)
2. they (doors)
3. it (door)
4. I (Alice)
5. You (Alice)
6. her (Alice)
7. thou (David)

EXERCISE 2

1. I
2. him
3. she
4. me
5. I
6. I
7. they
8. me
9. me
10. us
11. him
12. he

CHAPTER **15** REFLEXIVE AND EMPHASIZING PRONOUNS

EXERCISE

Reflexive Pronoun	Emphasizing
itself (1)	himself (4)
ourselves (2)	
itself (3)	

Note : Number in bracket refers to the corresponding sentence number.

CHAPTER **16** DEMONSTRATIVE, INDEFINITE & DISTRIBUTIVE PRONOUNS

EXERCISE

1. None - Indefinite
2. That - Demonstrative
3. That - Demonstrative
4. One - Indefinite
5. Some - Indefinite
6. either - Distributive
7. each - Distributive
8. other - Indefinite
9. such - Indefinite
10. those - Demonstrative

CHAPTER 17 RELATIVE PRONOUNS

EXERCISE 1

	Relative Pronoun	Case	Antecedent
1.	whose	Possessive	woman
2.	that	Nominative	Jack
3.	whose	Possessive	Sailors
4.	which	Accusative	books
5.	that	Nominative	rat
6.	which	Nominative	books
7.	that	Accusative	book
8.	who	Nominative	children
9.	that	Accusative	knife
10.	that	Accusative	knife

EXERCISE 2

1. whom	2. that	3. that	4. who	5. What
6. Who	7. What	8. what	9. What	10. who

EXERCISE 3

1. The child whom I saw yesterday is dead
2. Show the road that leads to Delhi.
3. Those boys who had been very lazy were kept it.
4. There you see the boy who bowls very well.
5. You spoke to the man who is deaf.
6. The boy who tells lies deserves to be punished.
7. I know a man who has a woodenleg.
8. The captain praised Balu, whose bowling was very good.
9. This is my cousin about whom I was speaking.
10. A man who came running up heard me calling.

EXERCISE 4

1. whom	2. who	3. who	4. whom	5. whom
6. whom	7. whom	8. whom	9. whom	10. whom

EXERCISE 5

1. has - one of the mothers (singular)
2. has - the first man (singular)

3. come - one of his best traits (singular)
4. was - one of the songs (singular)
5. kills - one of the things (singular)
6. was - one of the stories (singular)
7. is - one of those passions (singular)
8. prevents - delicacy of ideas (singular)
9. tends; itself - Tyranny (singular)

CHAPTER 18 INTERROGATIVE PRONOUNS

EXERCISE

1. Who	2. Whom	3. Which	4. Which	5. Who
6. Whom	7. Which	8. What	9. What	10. What

CHAPTER 19 THE VERB

EXERCISE 1

Intransitive Verb :

1. stopped	3. rises	4. ticks	5. looked	7. lies
9. eat	10. hopped	12. sat	17. fell	

Transitive Verb : Object

2. blew – whistle
6. put – books
8. changes – things
11. does not keep – time
18. shall bring — camera

Transitive Verb : Object

13. could not spare – time
14. lifted – weight
15. wrote – letter
16. know – man

EXERCISE 2

Transitive

1. I **saw** a girl.
2. She **ate** a mango.
3. The postman **gave** the letter.
4. Ram **drove** the car.
5. Boys **play** cricket.

Intransitive

1. Girls **are** in the ground.
2. They **were dancing**.
3. Dogs **are barking**.
4. Lazy people **go on speaking**.
5. Wise men never **talk**.

CHAPTER 20 LINKING VERBS

EXERCISE

Intransitive Verbs	Complement
1. roars	–
3. stood	on the burning deck
6. are out	–
7. tried	again
8. fell	asleep
9. hide	in the daytime
11. went	mad
12. waited	patiently
15. flew	down
16. looks	threatening
18. seems	true

Transitive Verbs	Object	Objective Complement
2. proved	'false'	–
5. saw	burning ship	–
10. hide	faults	–
13. elected	him	President
14. struck	remain	dead
15. stole	the cheese	–
17. made	him	General

CHAPTER 21 INTRODUCTION TO TENSES

EXERCISE

Verbs	Tense
1. flows	Simple Present
2. will answer	Simple Future
3. has been raining	Present Perfect Continuous
4. had finished	Past Perfect
5. have lived	Present Perfect
6. will have reached	Future Perfect
7. said	Simple Past
had finished	Past Perfect

8. will be flying   Future Continuous
9. was having   Past Continuous
10. have been waiting   Present Perfect Continuous

CHAPTER 23 — THE USES OF TENSES : TALKING ABOUT THE PRESENT & PAST

EXERCISE 1

1. goes   2. is coming   3. has   4. boils
5. belongs   6. is boiling   7. go   8. is tapping
9. wants   10. are playing

EXERCISE 2

1. I got up at 6 A.M.
2. I had tea with my relatives at 7 A.M.
3. I watched the morning programme on T.V.
4. We had lunch at 1 P.M.
5. I had a little nap between 2 and 3 P.M.

EXERCISE 3

1. has repaired   2. have known
3. have closed   4. have visited
5. have paid   6. have trod or trodden

EXERCISE 4

Example { (A) Have you ever seen the Taj?
         (B) Yes, I have seen it several times. No, I have never seen it.

1. (A) Have you ever been to Kashmir ?
   (B) Yes, I have twice been to Kashmir. No, I have never been to Kashmir.

2. (A) Have you ever phoned her ?
   (B) Yes, I have phoned her several times. No, I have never phoned her.

3. (A) Have you ever lived in Jaipur?
   (B) Yes, we have lived in Jaipur for five years.
        No, we have never lived in Jaipur.

4. **(A)** Have you ever seen a Hindi film?

   (B) Yes, we have seen several times.

   No, we have never seen a Hindi film.

5. **(A)** Have you ever drunk the Camel's milk.

   (B) Yes, I have drunk the Camel's milk on two or three occasions.

   No, I have never drunk the Camel's milk.

6. **(A)** Have you ever visited Mahabalipuram?

   (B) Yes, we have visited many times. No, we have never visited.

EXERCISE 5

1. saw	2. have known	3. have closed
4. have had	5. have solved	6. visited

EXERCISE 6

Make 'How long...?' Questions.

1. How long have you been learning English?

   I have been learning English since four years.

2. How long have you been learning grammar?

   We have been learning grammar for three years.

3. How long have you been reading this book?

   I have been reading this book since 7 o'clock.

4. How long have you been wearing these clothes?

   We have been wearing these clothes since yesterday.

5. How long have you been doing this exercise?

   I have been doing this exercise since 5 P.M.

6. How long have you been living in this city?

   We have been living in this city for seven years.

EXERCISE 7

1. Saroja **had burnt** her hand while she **was cooking** the dinner.

2. Anil came at 10:30. You **had gone** to bed by that time.

3. Gopi **fell** asleep while he **was reading** the magazine.

4. We **got** to the cinema late, so the film **had** already **started**.

5. The boy **fell** while he **was running**.

6. He **had felt** very tired because he **was playing** football for two hours.

CHAPTER 24 THE USES OF TENSES : TALKING ABOUT THE FUTURE

EXERCISE

1. The train **leaves** at 8:20.
2. We **are going** to Hyderabad tomorrow.
3. It is late. I think I **am going** to bed now.
4. "Who is arranging the party? Mohan **will do** it.
5. "Tea or Coffee?" I will **have** coffee.
6. I **will be flying** to Delhi at this time tomorrow.
7. The boat is full of water. It **will sink**.

CHAPTER 25 AUXILIARY AND MODAL VERBS

EXERCISE

Verb Modal	Permission	ability	possibility	certainty	obligation	request	offer	suggestion
can	✓	✓				✓		
could	✓	✓	✓			✓		
may	✓		✓					
might			✓					
will					✓		✓	
would					✓		✓	
shall						✓	✓	✓
should					✓		✓	✓
must					✓			
ought					✓			necessity

CHAPTER 26 VERB FORMS IN CONDITIONALS

EXERCISE

1. will get
2. had
3. would accept
4. comes
5. had invited
6. would have met

CHAPTER 27 ACTIVE AND PASSIVE VOICE

EXERCISE 1

Active	Passive
see (1)	was obeyed (2)
struck (2)	had been damaged (3)
takes (3)	will be gained (4)
	was posted (6)
	has been repaired (7)
	was lost (9)
	has been posted (10)

Note : Number in bracket refers to the corresponding sentence number.

EXERCISE 2

1. The mouse was killed by the cat.
2. The tree was cut down by the man.
3. He was praised by the teacher.
4. The programme has been videoed by them.
5. A kite was being made of murder by Rama.
6. A letter will be written by my father.
7. He will be conquered by me.
8. I was kept waiting by him.
9. The ball was thrown by Sohrab.
10. Twenty runs were scored by him.

EXERCISE 3

1. My name was asked by them.
2. Admission was refused.
3. The ocean cannot be pumped dry.
4. He was found guilty of murder by them.
5. Often milk is turned sour by a thunder storm.
6. The storm was seen approaching.

EXERCISE 4

1. Latiff didn't speak a word.
2. His friends took him to the hospital.
3. His singular appearance struck me.
4. Everyone will blame us.

5. This did not surprise Alice.
6. It will greatly surprise him if they choose him.

EXERCISE 5

Active Voice	Passive Voice
1. Rama killed Ravana.	Ravana was killed by Rama.
2. Smoking will spoil his health.	His health will be spoiled by smoking.
3. It had brought him to the street.	He had been brought to the street by it.

EXERCISE 6

1. Balu was elected captain.   2. He was seen opening the box.
3. His words must be listened to.   4. Who broke this jug?
5. Will those happy days ever be forgotten?

CHAPTER 28 MOOD

EXERCISE

Indicative Mood : 1, 6, 9
Imperative Mood : 2, 3, 5, 7, 10
Subjunctive Mood : 4, 8

CHAPTER 29 AGREEMENT OF THE VERB WITH THE SUBJECT

EXERCISE 1

1. He with his father was among the first to arrive. **Singular subject** 'He'
2. Their lives, their liberties, and their religion are in danger.

lives, liberties, religion – **Plural.**

3. Mr. Smith with his wife and children live next door.

Singular subject – Mr. Smith

4. The fleet is under orders to sail.

Collective noun takes a singular verb.

EXERCISE 2

1. is   2. has   3. are   4. was

CHAPTER **30** **THE INFINITIVE**

CHAPTER **30** **THE INFINITIVE**

EXERCISE 1

1. to fight - object of a preposition (but - except)
2. to advance - qualify a noun (order)
3. to forgive - qualify a verb 'is'
4. to scoff - complement of a verb 'came'
   to pray - complement of a verb 'remained'
5. to relieve - subject of 'was'
6. to blush - complement 'is born'
7. to soothe - qualify a verb 'hath'
8. to retreat - subject of 'was'
   to advance - subject of 'was'
9. to enjoy - object of 'wishes'
10. to be lost - qualify a Noun 'moment'

EXERCISE 2

1. Every cricket team has a captain to direct the other players.
2. You must part with your purse to save your life.
3. His father went to Ajmer yesterday to visit the shrine of the saint Khwaja Pir.
4. He works hard to earn his livelihood.
5. The insolvent property was sold by the official Assignee to pay the insolvent's creditors.
6. The strikers held a meeting to discuss the terms of the employers.
7. England expects everyone to do his duty.
8. He must apologise for his misconduct to escape punishment.

CHAPTER **31** **THE PARTICIPLE**

EXERCISE 1

Present Participle

1. pouring - modified by an adverb 'down'
2. being - qualified by an adjective 'weary'
4. being - qualified by an adjective 'occupied'

5. coming - used attributively
8. seeing - used predicatively

Past Participle
3. broken - adjective
6. read - adjective
7. learned - adjective; forgotten - Passive voice

EXERCISE 2

1. The porter, on opening the gate, we entered.
2. Starting early, we arrived at noon.
3. We met a man carrying a load of wood.
4. Being the stable door open, the horse was stolen.
5. On seizing his stick he rushed to the door.
6. Taking up his gun the hunter went out to shoot.
7. Having stolen a piece of cheese, the crow flew to her nest to enjoy the tasty meal.
8. The wolf having wished to pick up a quarrel with the lamb said how dare it make the water muddy.
9. Alighting from the train a passenger fell over a bag on the platform.
10. Meeting his brother in the street Nanak asked him where he was going.
11. Being charmed with the silk, my sister bought ten yards.
12. Being delayed by a storm the streamer came into port a day late.
13. Having resolved on a certain course, he acted with vigour.
14. Staggering back he sank to the ground.
15. The letter, being badly written, I had great difficulty in making out its contents.
16. A hungry fox saw some bunches of grapes hanging from a vine.

EXERCISE 3

1. Weary of travelling the destination seemed a hundred miles away.
2. On information he was arrested for complicity in the plot.
3. Under a cool shelter, the hours were beguiled with desultory talk.
4. An old temple was seen up the hill.
5. The fog was very dense nothing could be seen.
6. We hope to hear from you soon. Yours sincerely.
7. Called upon him yesterday, he subscribed a handsome sum to the Relief Fund.

CHAPTER **32** THE GERUND

EXERCISE

1. fighting - Participle - 'life' noun
2. reading - Gerund - Subject of a verb
3. hearing - Gerund - Subject of a verb
4. standing – Participle – 'clown' Noun
5. Asking, answering – Gerund – Subject of a verb
6. Waving – Gerund absolutely
7. Walking – subject
8. Jumping – Participle
9. hoarding – Gerund - absolutely
10. returning – after a preposition
11. Amassing – subject of a verb
12. being – after a preposition
13. playing – Gerund – absolutely
14. spending – object
15. having – Gerund, object

CHAPTER **33** THE SEQUENCE OF TENSES

EXERCISE 1

1. was	2. was	3. could	4. will	5. continued
6. like	7. have repented		8. was limping	
9. come	10. might			

EXERCISE 2

1. would	2. would	3. could	4. could	5. would
6. could	7. would	8. could		

CHAPTER **34** THE ADVERB

EXERCISE 1

Adverb	Modifies	Kinds of Adverbs
1. So	modifies the Adjectives 'glad'	Adv. of Degree
2. too	modifies the Adjectives 'many'	Adv. of Degree

3. well   modifies the Verb 'well'   Adv. of Manner
4. once, twice   modifies the Verb 'have met'   Adv. of Frequency
5. off   modifies the Adverb 'far'   Adv. of Place
6. surely   modifies the Verb 'expect'   Adv. of Manner
7. so   modifies the Adj. 'angry'   Adv. of Manner
8. too   modifies the Adv. 'far'   Adv. of Manner
9. differently   modifies the Verb 'see'   Adv. of Manner
   now   modifies the Verb 'see'   Adv. of Time
10. closely   modifies the Verb 'crowd'   Adv. of Place
    so   modifies the Adv. 'closely'   Adv. of Manner

EXERCISE 2

Adverb	Adjective
Lalitha is **very** badly ill.	This is the **very** first time he visits.
He has **nearly** paid the dues.	You are too **near**.
Somu is **ill**-advised	She has an **ill**-feeling
Only you could do that.	He is the **only** soldier I know.
The rope was cut **clean** through.	She wrote on a **clean** paper.
Have you been here **long**?	It was a **long** journey.
The train is an hour **late**.	The **late** chairman is living abroad.
The bus arrived **early**.	It is an **early** train.
The horse runs **fast**.	The mud was stuck **fast** to my shoes.

CHAPTER **35** **COMPARISON OF ADVERBS**

EXERCISE

Adverbs	Comparative	Superlative
suddenly	more suddenly	most suddenly
often	more often	most often
near	nearer	nearest
loud	louder	loudest
hard	harder	hardest
wisely	more wisely	most wisely
patiently	more patiently	most patiently

CHAPTER 36 POSITION OF ADVERBS

EXERCISE

1. The two brothers are **nearly** alike.
2. I came **merely** to return a book.
3. There were **only** three or four boys late.
4. **Really** I did not want to come.
5. He **often** invited me to visit him.
6. I am **never** determined to yield this point.

CHAPTER 37 ADVERB PHRASES

EXERCISE 1

1. That boy works energetically.
2. I will be with you shortly.
3. He suffered patiently.
4. He met his misfortune courageously.
5. I accept your statement unreservedly.

EXERCISE 2

1. We have to earn **at all costs**.
2. He shouted **at the top of his voice**.
3. He started **in a hurry**.
4. The cooks do everything **to my satisfaction**.
5. I have kept all the documents **under lock and key**.
6. He left that job **for good**.
7. She has spent her days **in good time**.
8. **In the long run** they became good friends.
9. You have to do this job **without fail**.

CHAPTER 38 THE PREPOSITION

EXERCISE 1

1. in – governs the word 'corner'
2. to – governs the word 'cupboard'
3. for – governs the word 'crown'
4. of – governs the word 'rooks'; over – governs the word 'head'

5. of – governs the word 'credit'
6. into – governs the word 'street'
7. beside – governs the word 'hill'
8. around – governs the word 'porch'
9. of – governs the word 'life'; without – governs the word 'name'
10. out – governs the word 'fears'

EXERCISE 2

Prepositions	Adverb
We are right **behind** you.	I left my hat **behind** at work.
You have to go **up** the stairs.	Eat **up** your dinner.
They were sitting **by** the fire.	I walked **by**.
We walked **along** the road.	Would to like to come **along**.
He is working **in** Kolkata.	Is the train **in** yet?
What is this book **about**?	He is somewhere **about**.
He spends **beyond** his means.	I saw a cottage **beyond**.
I work **under** the owner of the factory.	I travel **under** a false name.
You have to be present **before** 2 o'clock.	I have never seen her **before**.
He asked **after** you.	The street was named **after** her.

EXERCISE 3

1. along	2. under	3. to, on	4. over	5. at
6. off	7. for	8. by, with	9. by	10. about

EXERCISE 4

1. at, on	2. to, by	3. at	4. by, in	5. at, on, to
6. within	7. since	8. at	9. to	10. at, from
11. between	12. by	13. at, in	14. Since	15. Besides
16. in	17. with	18. beside	19. of	20. by, with

CHAPTER 39 THE CONJUNCTION

EXERCISE 1

Co-ordinating Conjunctions :

3. or	6. whether	7. for	8. or

Subordinating Conjunctions :

1. because   2. if   4. than   5. unless

EXERCISE 2

A.

1. Prasad is studious, **but** not successful.
2. It is raining. Take **either** a raincoat **or** an umbrella.
3. **Neither** Krishnan **nor** Murali is in U.S.A.
4. I do not care **whether** you help me **or** not.

B.

1. Please inform **that** I will visit them in June.
2. Procure enough money **before** you begin the construction.
3. I know **how** to make it a successful one.
4. **As** Elumalai is sick he is not able to write the examination.
5. **Unless** you word hard you cannot succeed.
6. Please wait here **until** I bring my car.
7. **Though** the mason came late he finished the job.
8. **When** I was in my village, I knew nothing about Madras.
9. Make hay **while** the sun shines.
10. Varan joined his friend **where** his friend stayed.
11. **If** he is a good plumber, he will do this properly.
12. Kumar likes his friend better **than** his brother.

EXERCISE 3

1. and   2. but   3. or
4. unless   5. since   6. till

EXERCISE 4

Adverb	Preposition	Conjunction
before (2)	before (1)	before (3)
since (4)	since (5)	

CHAPTER 41 THE INTERJECTION

EXERCISE

A.

1. Hello! come here. Watch the programme.
2. Alas! he has missed the catch.
3. Hush! Don't shout.

Note : Number in bracket refers to the corresponding sentence number.

4. Ah! has he caught.

5. Hurrah! we have won the game.

CHAPTER 42 — THE SAME WORD USED AS DIFFERENT PARTS OF SPEECH

EXERCISE

Adjective	Adverb	Preposition	Conjunction
much (1)	much (3)	After (6)	after (8)
much (2)	about (5)	after (10)	
little (4)	best (11)	but (15)	
after (7)	best (13)		
best (12)	after (9)		
	but (14)		

Note : Number in bracket refers to the corresponding sentence number.

CHAPTER 43 — WORDS FOLLOWED BY APPROPRIATE PREPOSITIONS

EXERCISE 1

1. for, of   2. to   3. to, for   4. at, for   5. by, towards

6. with, to   7. to, for   8. down, of   9. for, in, in   10. with, of

EXERCISE 2

1. from, between, in, for   2. with, about, at, in, for

3. from, for, for   4. for, to, from

5. of, against   6. in, of

7. to, with, among

EXERCISE 3

1. in, with   2. of, about, to   3. in, for, with   4. from, to, with

5. over, for, of, on   6. of, in, from   7. with, on   8. for, to

CHAPTER 44 — PUNCTUATION

EXERCISE 1

1. Even a fool, when holdeth his peace is counted wise.

2. I therefore walked back, by the horse way, which was five miles round.

3. Read not to contradict, nor to believe, but to weigh and consider.

4. When we have dined, to prevent the ladies leaving us, generally ordered the table to be removed.

5. Rabindranath Tagore, the another of **Gitanjali**, was the first Asian to win the Nobel Prize.

EXERCISE 2

1. They had played together in infancy; they had worked together in man hood; they were now tottering about and gossiping away the evening of life and in a short time they will probably be buried together in the neighbouring churchyard.

2. "My quaint, Ariel", said Prospero to the little spirite, when he made him free. "I shall miss you, yet you shall have your freedom." "Thank you my dear master," said Ariel, "but give me leave to attend your ship home, with prosperous gales, before you bid farewell to the assistance of your, faithful spirit."

3. The shepherd finding his flock destroyed, exclaimed, "I have been rightly served; why did I trust my sheep to a wolf."

4. "As Caesar loved me, I wept for him; as he was fortunate, I rejoice at it; as he was valiant, I honour him, but as he was ambitious, I slew him."

5. Sancho ran as fast as his ass could go to help his master, whom he found lying and not able to stir such a blow. "He and Rozinante had received mercy on me", cried Sancho "Did I not give your worship fair warning ? Did I not tell you they were wind-mills and that nobody could think otherwise, unless he had also wind-mills in his head."

6. "Perhaps" cried he, "there may be such monsters as you describe."

7. "Take away that bauble" said Cromwell, pointing to the mace which lay upon the table and when the House was empty, he went out with the key in his pocket.

8. One day walking together up the hill, I said to Friday, "Do you not wish yourself in your own country a gain." "Yes" he said "what would you do there?" said I. "Would you turn wild and eat men's flesh again?" He looked full of concern and shaking his head said, "No, no."

9. "Wretch," said the king, "what harm did I do thee, that, thou shouldst seek to take my life with your own hand! "You killed my father and my two brothers," was the reply.

10. Androcles, who had no arms of any kind, now gave himself up for lost. "What shall I do?" said he. "I have no spear or sword, no, not so much as a stick, to defend myself with."

11. When a great office is vacant, either by death or disgrace, which often happens. Five or six of these candidates petition the emperor to entertain his majesty and the court with a dance on the rope; and whoever jumps the highest without falling succeeds to the office.

CHAPTER 45	ANALYSIS OF SIMPLE SENTENCES

EXERCISE

Subject			Predicate			
Simple Subject	Attribute (Enlargement)	Verb	Complement	Object	Attribute (Enlargement)	Adverbial Adjunct (Extension)
1. God		tempers	to the shorn lamb	the wind		
2. It		is	to live in suspense	thing	a miserable	
3. Wounds	made by words	are	to heal			
4. Work and play	all no	makes		Jack	a dull boy	
5. A man he		was	to all the country dear			
6. Experience		has taught		us many lessons		
7. He		showed		solicitude	a constant	for his son's welfare
8. Caesar	having conquered his enemies	returned				to Rome
9. It		is	to be wise			easy, after the event.
10. Fortune	a great	is	a great misfortune			in the hands of a fool

CHAPTER 47	CLAUSE ANALYSIS OF COMPLEX SENTENCES

EXERCISE

Clause	Kind of Clause	Connective
1. **A.** I had a partial father –	Principal clause.	
B. who gave me a better education –	sub. Adj. clause qualifying 'father' in A	
C. than his broken fortune would been allowed	sub. Adv. clause modifying 'better' in B	
2. **A.** The man is a fool	Principal clause	
B. who does not see	Sub. Adj. Clause qualifying 'fool' in A	
C. that the good of every living creature is his good	sub. Noun clause Subordinate to B of 'see'	'that' connective
3. **A.** He told us –	Principal clause.	
B. but he had read Milton in a prose translation	Sub. Noun Clause subordinate to 'A' object of 'told'	Connective 'that'
C. when he was fourteen.	Sub. Adv. clause of time subordinate to 'B'	connective 'when'
4. **A.** I determined to send him to town	Principal Clause	
B. as my eldest son was bred a scholar	Sub. Adv. Clause of reason subordinate to 'A' modifying 'determined'.	As
C. where his abilities might contribute to our support and his own	Sub. Adv. clause of place Subordinate to 'A' modifying 'town'	when
5. **A.** Nothing can describe the confusion of thought	Principal Clause	
B. which I felt	Sub. Adj. Clause qualify 'thought'	
C. when I sank into the water	Sub. Adv. Clause of 'place' modifying 'felt' in 'B'	when
6. **A.** We are not to be surprised	Principal Clause	
B. considering that the world is so intricate	Sub. Noun Clause subordinate to 'A' object of 'surprised'	that
C. that science progressed slowly	Sub. Noun Clause, subordinate to 'A' object of 'surprised'	that

Contd.

7. **A.** We had in this village, some twenty years ago, an idiot boy	Principal Clause	
B. whom I well remember	Sub. Adj. Clause subordinate to 'boy'	
C. who from a child showed a strong propensity for bees	Sub. Adj. Clause qualifying 'boy' in 'A'	connective
8. **A.** He will always find his happiness incomplete	Principal Clause	
B. with whatever luxuries a bachelor may be surrounded	Sub. Noun clause, object to 'will find'	
C. unless he has a wife and children	Sub. Adv. Clause of condition, subordinate to 'B' modify 'may be surrounded'	unless
9. **A.** one of the first is	Principal Clause	
B. that I read Shakespeare in my mother tongue	Sub. Noun Clause object of 'is'	that
C. Among the many reasons which make me glad to have been born in England	Sub. Adj. Clause qualify 'first' (reason) in 'A'	among
10. **A.** He (Pope) professed to have learned his poetry from Dryden	Principal Clause	
B. whom he praised through his whole life with unvaried liberality	Sub. Adj. Clause qualify 'Dryden' in A.	
C. whenever an opportunity was presented	Sub. Adv. Clause modifying 'preferred' to in 'A'	whenever
11. **A.** Milton said	Principal Clause	
B. that he did not educate his daughters in the languages	Sub. Noun Clause object to 'said' in A	that
C. because one tongue was enough for a woman	Sub. Adv. of reason modifying the verb 'did not educate'	because
12. **A.** We hardly realise	Principal Clause	
B. who are fortunate enough to live in this enlightened century.	Sub. Adj. Clause qualifying 'We' in A.	
C. how our ancestors suffered from their belief in the existence of mysterious and malevolent beings.	Sub Adj. Clause of manner, modify the verb 'realize' in B	
13. **A.** We cannot agree with Dr. Johnson	Principal Clause	
B. much as we like Shakespeare's comedies	Sub. Adv. Clause of reason, modify the verb 'agree' in A	
C. that they are better than his tragedies	Sub. Adv. Clause of degree B, modifying 'much' in B.s	

Contd.

14. A. Those will find	Principal Clause	
B. who look into practical life	Sub. Adj. Clause qualifies 'those' in A	
C. that fortune is usually on the side of the industrious	Sub. Noun Clause object of 'will find'	
D. as the wind and waves are on the side of the best navigators	Sub. Adv. Clause of comparison modifying 'is'	as
15. A. History says	Principal Clause	
B. that Socrates continued to talk to the friends	Sub. Noun Clause object of 'says'	that
C. when he was given the cup of hemlock	sub. Adv. Clause of time modifying 'continued'	when
D. who were standing around him	Sub. Adj. Clause qualifying 'friends'	who
E. as he drank it	Sub. Adv. Clause of time modifying 'given'	as
16. A. He hardly knows	Principal Clause	
B. who sits from day to day	Sub. Adj. Clause qualifying 'He'	
C. where the prisoned lark is hung	Sub. Adv. Clause modify 'knows'	
D. that it has sung	Sub. Noun Clause object of that 'knows'	

CHAPTER 48 — CLAUSE ANALYSIS OF COMPOUND SENTENCES

EXERCISE

A. Clause	Kind of clause	Connective
1. A. God called to Abraham	Main Clause coordinate with B	Connect
B. and asked him	Main Clause coordinate with A	and
C. when the old man was gone	Sub. Adv. Clause of time modifying 'asked'	
D. where the stranger was	Sub. Adv. Clause of place	
2. A. And be not melancholy	Main Clause coordinate with B	
B. and wish yourself in heaven	Main clause Coordinate with A	

C. while you are upon Earth	Sub. Adv. Clause modifying the verb 'enjoy'	
D. enjoy the good things	Main Clause	that
E. that are here	Sub. Adj. Clause qualifying 'things'	
3. A. There is no saying	Main Clause	
B. that shocks me so much as that	sub. Adj. Clause qualifying 'saying'	that
C. which I hear very often	Main Clause coordinate with A	
D. that a man does not know	Main Clause coordinate with C	that
E. how to pass his time	Sub. Adv. Clause of manner modifying 'does not know'	how
4. A. Mr. Burchell had scarce taken leave	Main Clause coordinate with B	
B. (And) Sophia consented to dance with the chaplain	Main Clause coordinate with A.	
C. when my little ones came running out to tell us	Sub. Adv. Clause of time modifying 'came'	when
D. that the squire has come with a crowd of company	Sub. Noun Clause object of 'To tell'	
5. A. He replied	Main Clause	
B. I trust him away	Sub-Noun Clause object to 'replied'	
C. because he did not worship thee	Sub. Adj. Clause of time modifying 'replied'	because
6. A. All have done good work	Main Clause coordinates with C	
B. who have meant good work with their whole hearts	Sub. Adj. Clause qualifying 'All'	
C. although they may die	Main Clause coordinates with A 'although'	
D. before they have the time to sign it	Main Clause coordinates with C	'before'
7. A. the parrot took a sudden dislike to him	Main Clause coordinates with B	
B. and chased him in and out of the rooms	Main Clause coordinates with A	
C. while the people looked on	Sub. Adv. Clause of manner modifying 'Chased'	
D. and applauded the parrot's agility	Main Clause coordinates with C	And

Contd.

8. A. One day Bassanio came to Antonio.	Main Clause coordinates with B
B. and told him	Main Clause coordinates with A
C. that he wished to repair his fortune by a wealthy marriage with a lady	Sub. Noun Clause Object of told
D. whom he dearly loved	Sub. Adj. Clause qualifying 'lady'
E. whose father had left her sole heiress to a large estate.	Sub. Adj. Clause qualifying 'lady'

CHAPTER 49 TRANSFORMATION OF SENTENCES

EXERCISE 1

1. He speaks so fast that it cannot be understood.
2. He is so ignorant that he cannot be a postman.
3. He is so proud that he cannot beg.
4. She was sobbing so deeply that she could not make any answer.
5. It is never so late that it cannot be mended.
6. This tree is so high that I cannot climb.

EXERCISE 2

1. (a) If you beware of pick-pockets there will be no further trouble.
   (b) Unless you beware of pick-pockets there will be trouble.
   (c) Provided you beware of pick-pockets there will be further trouble.
2. (a) Provided he is not shy, he would certainly have made his mark as a speaker.
   (b) If he is not shy, he would certainly have made his mark as a speaker.
   (c) In case he is not shy, he would certainly have made his mark as a speaker.
3. (a) Should you have been less rash, the consequences would not have been so serious.
4. (a) Unless he is seriously ill, I will not wire you.
   (b) Provided he is not seriously ill, I will not wire you.
5. (a) If a taxi is not available, a cab will do.
   (b) In case a taxi is not available, a cab will do.

6. (a) Provided you did not make that unfortunate remark the conference would not have ended in a fiasco.

7. (a) I will buy the horse if it is quite sound.

    (b) Provided the horse is quite sound I will buy it.

    (c) Supposing the horse is quite sound I will buy it.

8. (a) Had you resisted the first temptation, the next will be easier to overcome.

    (b) Resist the first temptation and the next will be easier to overcome.

9. (a) If you are anxious to make money, buy these shares.

    (b) Unless you are not anxious to make money, don't buy these shares.

10. (a) Unless there are plenty of money, everybody would care for it.

    (b) Provided that money was in plenty, nobody would care for it.

EXERCISE 3

1. (a) Though I pay the man much, he is never satisfied.

    (b) Admitting that I pay the man much he is never satisfied.

    (c) Inspite of paying the man much he is never satisfied.

2. (a) Although he is his brother, he does not resemble him.

    (b) Inspite of being his brother, he does not resemble him.

3. (a) Notwithstanding that he began late, he finished first.

4. Though he has hardly any chance, I shall use my influence on his behalf.

5. His father still trusted him in spite of having deceived by him.

6. He is a kind-hearted man though he has his weaknesses.

7. In spite of being maliciously criticised, he never showed any ill-will to those who persecuted him.

8. In spite of madness there is method in it.

EXERCISE 4

1. Very few kings were as great as Akbar.	**Positive**
Akbar was greater than most other kings.	**Comparative**
2. No other woman was as beautiful as Helen of Troy.	**Positive**
3. Latiff is more industrious than most other boys.	**Comparative**
Latiff is one of the most industrious boy of all.	**Superlative**
4. Very few Indian kings were so great as Samudra Gupta.	**Positive**
Samudra Gupta was greater than most other Indian kings.	**Comparative**
5. He would die soon than tell a lie.	**Positive**

6. This newspaper has the biggest circulation of all.   **Superlative**
   No other morning paper has so big a circulation as this.   **Positive**
7. Few people have as much money as brains.   **Positive**
8. A foolish friend is not so good as a wise enemy.   **Positive**
9. Ooty is healthier than any other hill sanitarium in India. **Comparative**
10. Mahatma Gandhi was greater than most other men in the world.

                                                               Comparative
   Very few men in the world are as great as Mahatma Gandhi. **Positive**

EXERCISE 5

1. The first Crusade was preached by Peter the Hermit.
2. We were shown some ancient coins by the curator of the museum.
   Some ancient coins were shown to us by the curator of the museum.
3. Beasts are taught by nature to know their friends.
4. Four millions African slaves were emancipated by Lincoln.
5. With astonishment it will be learnt by the public that war is imminent.
6. It was hoped by Macbeth to succeed Duncan.
7. His voice will be heard no more.

EXERCISE 6

1. They have cut the telegraph wires.
2. We can gain nothing without effort.
3. Alexander Graham Bell invented the telephone.
4. Everyone will blame us.
5. His singular appearance struck me.
6. They chose him leader.
7. Who broke him jug?
8. They pronounced harsh sentences on the offenders.

EXERCISE 7

1. The rose by no other name would not smell as sweet.
2. I will never hate the hills of the highlands.
3. None, but a millionaire can afford such extravagance.
4. No other democracy in the world is as large as India.
5. I don't own any other wealth except these fishing nets.

EXERCISE 8

1. I am little tired.
2. Everyone present cheered him.

3. We found the road good.
4. The two brothers are alike.
5. He has promised to avoid wine.

EXERCISE 9

1. Anyone who touches pitch gets defiled.
2. If you can think you can add cubit to his statue.
   No man can add a cubit to his stature by taking thought.
3. It does not matter much though the field be lost.
4. That is not the way a gentleman should behave.
5. Everybody knows the owl.

EXERCISE 10

1. How can one be expected to submit for ever to injustice?
2. Is there anything better than a busy life?
3. Will you find any where in the world a fairer building than the Taj Mahal?
4. It is useful to offer bread to a man who is dying of thirst?
5. Could we have not done anything with your help?
6. Was that an example to be followed?

EXERCISE 11

1. I would give you anything to see you happy.
2. There was a great fall my countrymen.
3. A quiet life affords a very sweet delight.
4. These mangoes have a delicious flavour.
5. It is quite shameful on your part to have so used a poor cripple.
6. It is not for a draught of ice-cold water.

EXERCISE 12

1. Oh! what a horrible night it is!
2. Alas! it was extremely base of him to desert you in your time of need.
3. Unbelievable ! How could he do such a thing.
4. How I wish, I had met you ten years ago.
5. How stupid it is of me to forget your name!
6. What an unhappy life he leads!

EXAMPLE 13

A.

1. Steel is strengthened by the addition of nickel.
2. He agreed to supply me with fire wood.
3. He rejected all that we proposed.
4. What he proposed is not clear from his letter.
5. You cannot be admitted without a ticket.
6. He does not intend of leaving the city.

B.

1. This scene surpasses the other beauties.
2. The defenders succeeded in repelling every attack on the city.
3. He has been admitted as the greatest general of the century.
4. They were overjoyed to welcome the good news.

C.

1. Though the ant is small its intelligence is like an elephant.
2. His action in his old age got everybody's admiration.
3. He said he has regrets for his haste action
4. Before I pay you your dues, you must affix your signature on this receipt.
5. The best way to be healthy is to control one's temperament.

D.

1. It is probable that the day will be fine.
2. The rats are a very troublesome.
3. He was dismissed as he was negligible rather than incompetent.
4. His cleverness was admitted, but his lacking industry was evident.
5. The merchant was successful in all his dealings, it was so natural that he was esteemed by his fellow citizens.

E.

1. She dressed poorly and meanly.
2. He did not break the rules intentionally, but it does not follow punishment wrongly.
3. Evidently it was his mistake, so was obviously his sincerity.
4. If you analyse these substances carefully, you will see they essentially differ.

CHAPTER 50 TRANSFORMATION OF SENTENCES (Contd.)

EXERCISE 1

1. She was dissatisfied and resigned his position.
2. He rushed against Horatius and smote him with all his might.
3. Evidently it was his mistake, so was obviously his sincerity.
4. The fog was very dense so the bus arrived very late.
5. The poet sat in his tower and gazed on the sea.
6. He had all his learning, but he was far from being a pedant.
7. Little Jack Horner sat in a corner and ate his Christmas pie.
8. The magician took pity on the mouse and turned it into a cat.
9. He has no fault of his own but he has become very poor.

EXERCISE 2

1. The children followed the piper.
2. Pushing his head into the tent the camel asked to be allowed to warm his nose.
3. In spite of being rich he is not contented.
4. Besides men, women and children were put to death.
5. Having never been to school the boy had no opportunity of learning to read or to write.
6. Besides not returning the goods he did not pay the bill.
7. By practising daily he became an expert player.
8. Having served out his sentence in gaol he was released.

EXERCISE 3

1. I cannot foretell the time when I will depart.
2. He pleaded that he was ignorant of the law.
3. He is said that he is a millionaire.
4. I shall be glad that you have advised me in this matter.
5. I overheard what he has remarked.
6. He believes that in that case it is certain for then to succeed.
7. Krishna wishes me that I should play for his team.

EXERCISE 4

1. The value of the exercise is as great as it could be.
2. The class room is not the place where the boys could play in.

3. He is hardly the boy who can do credit to school.
4. My friend who is the magistrate of this place is on leave.
5. Smoke which was the certain indicator of fire, appeared in the mine.
6. It was the work which was done by a wild animal.

EXERCISE 5

1. He replied as better as he can.
2. As he wanted to avoid waking his father he came in very quietly.
3. He has been partly blind since the time he had that illness.
4. Rama works harder than Krishna.
5. If I had no proper memory I can't tell you.
6. If you permit me I will go away.
7. Tiger is a fierce animal as everyone is feared by it.
8. I have issued order as the sanction was anticipated.

EXERCISE 6

1. The news is so good that it cannot be true.
2. He who lived in the island of Jamaica formerly was a very miserly planter.
3. One who succeeded went beyond his expectations.
4. He who went to bed, felt out of sorts.
5. An army of ants will attack animals that are large and ferocious.
6. He often gave his poor slaves very little food that they could not survive.
7. I love you still though you are full of faults.
8. Those who were the world's greatest men have not laboured to become rich.
9. He was so much excited that he cannot hear the reason.
10. A letter that brings to the club the news of Sir Roger's death is from the butler.
11. He is an habitual liar whose word cannot be trusted.
12. One who looks to the future is the prudent man.

EXERCISE 7

1. We hope for the better times.
2. The game was lost because of the consequence of his carelessness.
3. He asked the reason for my coming.
4. We believe his innocence.
5. As per the report, our troops have won a victory.
6. The prudent person is respected.

EXERCISE 8

1. The marks of the whip were visible.
2. A notorious idle boy was awarded the prize.
3. The translation of the Bible into English was the chief achievement for Wycliffe and his friends.
4. A dead man needs no riches.
5. Do you wish to say anything?
6. Do you not remember your former friend?

EXERCISE 9

1. He will pay you on hearing from me.

    or

    After he hears from me he will pay you.
2. Through all the countryside the tiger is renowned for its cunningness and ferocity.
3. I will support your action.
4. The horse is too old to work.
5. An honest man speaks his thought.

EXERCISE 10

1. The weather was too stormy for us to go.
2. Tell me your age.
3. I shall remain here.
4. Caesar, seeing Brutus among the Assassins covered his face with his gown.
5. Suspicion always haunts the mind of a culprit.

EXERCISE 11

1. Though the ship was wrecked, the crew were saved.
2. If you do your best you will never regret it.
3. He never tried again after he failed in his first attempt.
4. Though Rama may not be clever he is certainly industrious.
5. Although life has few enjoyments yet we cling to it.
6. You'll need few medicines if you eat few supper.
7. If you take care of the pence the pounds will take care of themselves.
8. If he had not run away they would have killed him.

EXERCISE 12

1. We had tried several and selected this bicycle.

2. Keep quiet or you will be punished

3. They went to war and extended their empire.

4. The Sky falls but he will not be frightened.

5. She was capricious and impertinent, but yet she was never out of temper.

6. I will be in better health and then I shall come.

EXERCISE 13

1. All the citizens turned to him in their perplexity because of his ability.

2. Before Bacon was sixteen he had finished his University studies.

3. He was ever engaged in the action which was the most perilous one.

4. The disaster was first reported terrible, latter it was turned out to be less terrible.

5. My expectations were quite less than what builder had done.

6. After he hears both sides he passes an opinion on any question.

EXERCISE 14

1. No sooner did the ship touch the shore than a soldier of the tenth legion leaped into the water.

2. Everyone of us has not only helped them with money but also with a body of well-trained and experienced workers.

3. Mrs. Smith is wiser than any body else in the family, while Jane is prettier than all her four daughters.

4. A special service devised for the occasion solved the difficulty.

5. The doctor compelled the lady to drink such vile medicine that he killed her.

6. His sole income is not what he earns by his pen.

7. (i) Only here a plane crashed last December.

   (ii) The plane was crashed here only last December.

8. In all probability his return is sure.

CHAPTER 51 SYNTHESIS OF SENTENCES

EXERCISE 1

1. The magician, taking pity on the mouse, turned into a cat.

2. Being warned of his danger the king made good escape.

3. Having hurried away with much haste Cinderalla dropped one of her little glass-slippers.
4. Having resolved on a certain course, he acted with vigour.
5. The Russians, having burnt Moscow, the French were forced to quit it.
6. On returning home, I saw a man looked very ill and lying by the roadside.

EXERCISE 2

1. Coal a very important mineral is hard, bright, black and brittle.
2. His only son, a lad of great promise died before him.
3. I love Bruno, my faithful dog.
4. The *Gitanjali*, Tagore's most famous work, is a collection of short poems.
5. Sardar Patel, a great stateman, the 'Iron Man of India' helped to unify India.

EXERCISE 3

1. I have examined the statement with many errors in it.
2. Even a bird will defend its young ones with great courage.
3. He set traps every night for clearing his house of rats.
4. It is impossible suspecting such a man of good record.
5. You helped me from drowning.
6. She stood there for hours without moving or speaking.

EXERCISE 4

1. Being a very hot day, I could not do my work satisfactorily.
2. Rain being plentiful this year rice is cheap.
3. The secretaryship being vacant I offered my service to undertake the duties of that post.
4. At sunrise, the fog having cleared the light house was seen less than a mile away.
5. The tiger sprang on his firing the gun and the ball gone high.
6. The boys made a lot of noise being the master out of the room and the door being shut.

EXERCISE 5

1. The information has come too take to use.
2. He is too poor to afford a car.
3. You were too prudent to invest all your saving to one concern.

4. Napoleon, the greatest of generals is universally acknowledged.
5. Various means were employed to kill Gulliver secretly by his majesty.
6. Some fierce dogs kept by him will guard his house from robbers.

EXERCISE 6

1. He was not at the meeting due to some unavoidable circumstances.
2. The blow dazed him only for the time being.
3. He expressed his regret by admitting his error.
4. The leave applied by him was not granted.
5. The growth of boys is very slow and invisible.
6. There was no reason for Rama striking Krishna cruelly and frequently.

EXERCISE 7

1. Ravindranth Tagore, founder of Shantiniketan, a Nobel Laureate was the author of the National Anthem.
2. He was able to talk to his friend in the next cell through a hole in the brick wall between the cell.
3. On hearing the drowning boy's shouts for help, a workman risking his own life plunged into the river.
4. The traveller toiling slowly over the desert turned round suddenly on hearing his companion's cry for help.
5. He wanted to make an example for them once and for all so he hardened his heart and punished the people mercilessly.
6. The enemy easily defeated the starving soldiers in rags and without ammunition or leaders.

CHAPTER **52** **SYNTHESIS OF SENTENCES (Contd.)**

EXERCISE

1. He does well but is nervous at the start.
2. He is both foolish and obstinate.

OR

He is foolish as well as obstinate.

3. You as well as Rama may go to the theatre.
4. No grains could be sown and a famine was feared for the monsoon failed and tanks became almost empty but the ryots looked anxiously for the next monsoon that proved unusually abundant and the danger was averted.

5. A husbandman had sown some corn in his field recently and cranes came to eat it but he had fixed a net to catch them.

OR

A husband man had fixed a net to eatch the eranes who came to eat the corn which he had sown in his field recently.

OR

Recently a husband man had sown some corn in his field and when the cranes came to eat it they were caught in the net.

6. The rain fell steadily for several days, and the river overflowed its banks and so the terrified villagers abandoned their homes to flee to the higher ground, but soon the floods retired and the villagers were able to return.

CHAPTER 53

SYNTHESIS OF SENTENCES (Contd.)

EXERCISE 1

1. Do you know the time when the train will arrive ?
2. I did not hear what he said.
3. Something that may be worth doing is only in doing well.
4. We don't know the number of enemy escaped.
5. Tell me where you have put my hat ?
6. It is a mystery how Subhash Chandra Bose died.
7. I cannot remember the place where I have seen this man.
8. I will show you how Columbus made an egg stand on its end.
9. I am very sorry that I cannot adequately express my sorrow.
10. I do not know when he will arrive.

EXERCISE 2

1. The man who committed the theft last night has been caught.
2. Can you tell me the reason why lately not keeping good health.
3. All of his plans of earning quick money failed.
4. A lion which was proud of his strength, despised the weakness of the mouse.
5. The fox saw the grapes which hung over the garden wall.
6. Mr. Haq, my travelling companion was an old gentleman whom I met in Basra.

EXERCISE 3

1. I could not sleep last night as it was very stuffy.
2. The nurse must be so tired as she had no sleep last night.
3. No other man in our community is as rich as him.
4. Arjun is as clever as Rama.
5. Since you are honest all will respect you.
6. Either you wish or not you must do the work.

EXERCISE 4

1. The doctor who attended him for years told me that though he lived very carefully he had very bad health which was inexplicable.
2. These facts should be kept in mind that the speed of the boat was remarkable, though it was going against the current and the wind.
3. Why he should worry as he is sure to receive his pay due to him.
4. Rama has declared his intention that he will not play against the Hindu school which is strong because he does not wish to tire himself before the cap-match which takes place on the next day.
5. A man should not pretend to be a doctor who is ignorant, had not learnt to read and write and could not even talk fluently.
6. I could prosecute them only if I know whom the sum is paid and for what reason.

EXERCISE 5

1. Though I offered him the needed help which he persisted in refusing and I left him to his fate.
2. As a fox saw a crow sitting on a tree with a piece of cheese, praised the crow's singing and pleased by the flattery, the crow began to sing, dropping the cheese.
3. A lion proud of his strength, despied the weakness of the mouse was caught in a net and could not escape, but was set free by the exertions of the mouse.
4. Running down the incline, the train attained great speed, turned a sharp curve at the bottom, oscillated under the infuence of the brakes and threw all the passengers into a panic.
5. A half-starved mouse managed to creep into a basket of corn, rejoiced in his good for fortune and then tried to get out of the basket but his body was too big to pass through the hole.

6. When she conducted me to her hut, she told me to remain there for the night and found me hungry, procured from outside, a fine fish, caused it to be half boiled upon some embers and then gave it to me for supper.

CHAPTER 54 DIRECT AND INDIRECT SPEECH

EXERCISE 1

1. He said that he had repeatedly warned/cautioned me not to play with fire.
2. The teacher remarked that we had all done it very badly.
3. They wrote that it was time they thought about settling that matter.
4. The teacher promised that he would explain that if they would come before school the next day.

OR

The teacher promised that if I would come before school the next day, he would explain that.

5. She wrote that she was waiting and watching and longing for her son's return.
6. The teacher promised that if I would come before school the next day, he would explain that
7. The dwarf said to her to promise him that when she was Queen, she would give him her first-born child.
8. He said that it was his horse and if he did not prove it in a few minutes he would give up his claim.
9. He cried that he would avenge his wrongs and he would not enter Athens until he had punished the king who had so cruelly treated him.
10. He wrote and said that he was unable to come just then because he was ill, but he would certainly start as soon as he was well enough to do so.

EXERCISE 2

1. He enquired how my father was.
2. The young Rakshas enquired into which way she went.
3. He asked her what she wanted.
4. Aladdin told the magician what he had done to deserve so severe a blow.
5. Ulysses asked the bird if it had anything to tell him.
6. The young sparrow enquired her mother what that queer object was.
7. They cried and enquired who he was and what he wanted.

8. Mr. Pickwick said, "I want to know why I and my friends have been brought here?"

EXERCISE 6

1. Goldsmith once said that he did not practise but he made it a rule to prescribe only for his friends.

   Beauclerk politely addressed the doctor as dear doctor and prayed him to alter his rule and prescribe only for his enemies.

2. Lady Grizzel exclaimed that she spoke French very well and Becky modestly replied that she ought to have known. She further added that she had taught that in a school and that her mother was a French-woman.

3. The Soldier asked the witch what she was going to do with the tinder-box. She him that it was no business of his and further added that he had got his money and command to give her back the tinder-box.

4. Nelson told Hardy that he was a dead man and was going fast and it would be all over with him soon. He (Nelson) requested him (Hardy) to come nearer to him and let his dear lady Hamilton have his hair and all other things belonging to him.

5. The judge enquired the litigants before him why didn't they settle the case out of the court. One of them said that was what they were doing when the police came and interferred

6. The hen bird was just about to lay and she said to her mate if he could not find her some place convenient for laying her eggs.

   He replied if that was not the very good place for the purpose.

   She answered in negative and said for it was continually overflowed by the tide.

   He exclaimed then if he was so feeble that the eggs laid in his house were to be carried away by the sea.

   The hen bird laughed and said that there was some considerable difference between he and the sea.

EXERCISE 3

1. The teacher commanded the boys to sit down.
2. The officer shouted to his men to halt.
3. The king ordered the Hatter to take off his hat.
4. The teacher advised him not to read so fast.
5. He said to me to wait until he came.
6. The swami told the villagers to bring him a drink of milk.
7. He ordered his servant to hurry up and not to waste time.
8. Their mother told the children to run away.
9. He instructed his daughter to take his golden jug and fetch him some water from the well.
10. His master ordered him to go down to the bazaar and bring him some oil and a lump of ice.

EXERCISE 4

1. Mr. Squeers sighed that milk was a rare article to be sure in London.
2. He angrily remarked that I was a stupid fellow.
3. He called upon God and said that he was ruined.
4. He exclaimed that their foes were too strong.
5. He complained that I was a lazy boy and I had done my work very badly.
6. She exclaimed that weather was awful.
7. He exclaimed that it was a nuisance.
8. He exclaimed angrily that it was so cruel of him.
9. He exclaimed sadly that he had not come.
10. The queen exclaimed sadly that he had done a rash and bloody deed.

EXERCISE 5

A.1. He said to Rama, "Please come with me."
2. Rama replied, "I cannot do so."
3. I wrote, "I will visit you tomorrow."
4. I said to them, "Be quite."
5. He said to me, "Have you anything to say?"
6. He advised his sons, "Do not quarrel amongst yourselves when I am dead but remain united."
7. The lion told the fox, "I am very weak, my teeth have fallen out and I have no appetite."